To Vic...

Thank you very
much for your
help!!
I hope you enjoy
this little travel
adventure keepsake!!
All the best!!

Linda Jaworski

Tellwell Talent
www.tellwell.ca

ISBN
978-0-2288-1622-5 (Hardcover)
978-0-2288-1621-8 (Paperback)
978-0-2288-1947-9 (eBook)

The Adventures of
DAN and DOVEE
in Italy

Linda Jaworski
Marilyn Smando
Illustrator: Linda Jaworski

"Wow, I've caught a huge fish," shouts Dan.

"Hey, that's no fish! It's a funny looking duck."

"My name is Dovee," sputters the duck, "and I am not a funny looking duck! I'm a special diving duck. Please get this hook out of my foot, whatever your name is!!"

"My name is Dan," says the boy. He takes the hook out of Dovee's foot.

"Are you OK? I can get my Mom to look at your foot."

"I'll just see if I can walk," says Dovee.

"Ouch!" says Dovee, as he stubs his foot on something.

Dan digs a bottle out of the sand.

"Wow, look at this," he says. "There's a treasure map inside the bottle!"

"...and there's something else inside the bottle," says Dan.

Dovee dumps out two mysterious-looking medallions on chains.

They immediately put on the medallions and blurt out, "We **wish** we could find the treasure!"

The medallions light up...

...and they find themselves in a fancy boat.

"Buon Giorno," says a man in the boat.

"What? Who are you and where are we?" asks Dan, feeling confused.

"Buon Giorno means 'good day' or 'hello' in Italian. I'm a gondolier who gives people rides in boats called gondolas. You are in Venice, Italy. Venice is the city of canals or waterways."

"Yeah!" says Dovee excitedly. "We are in Italy and this is the beginning of our treasure hunt adventure. Yippee!"

"Where's the map?" asks Dan.

"There it is at the bottom of the boat," says Dovee. "And what is this beside it? It's a puzzle piece with a picture of part of a map with a key attached."

"What is the key for?" asks Dan.

Dovee turns the puzzle piece over and they see a picture of a scooter with a message saying, "Look for this scooter in Venice."

"Please take us to a dock in Venice so we can get off the gondola," says Dan to the gondolier.

Dan and Dovee search for the scooter in Venice.

Canal in Venice

Rialto Bridge

Singing Gondolier

Church on San Giorgio Maggiore (Island)

Bridge of Sighs

VENICE

Carnival of Venice Costumes

Glass Blowing Studio

Saint Mark's Basilica

"Look! There's the scooter, Dan. It looks awesome! Let's check it out."

Gondolas at Dock

"Dovee, let's get on the scooter and see if the key fits."

"Yeah! It fits," says Dan.
"Now what?"

"I'm hungry! I **wish** we could have something to eat NOW," whines Dovee.

The medallions light up...

...and they find themselves in a big field seated at a table filled with food.

"Welcome to the Tuscany area of Italy, famous for its beautiful scenery," says a waiter. "We are just outside the city of Florence, Italy."

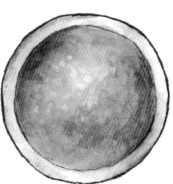

Pizza

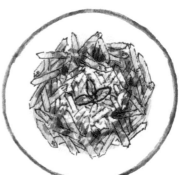

Penne Arrabiata

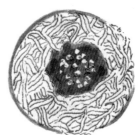

Spaghetti

Lasagna

"Dovee, you look so funny!!"

"Have you ever tried to eat spaghetti with a beak?!" questions Dovee.

The waiter hands Dan an envelope with another puzzle piece inside. The words on the back of this puzzle piece read: "Go through Florence and then to a place with a leaning tower."

So Dan and Dovee scoot off through Florence.

Uffizi Gallery

Cooking Class

Ponte Vecchio (Bridge)

Boboli Gardens

Museum in Palazzo Vecchio

Porcellino (Piglet Fountain)

Florence Cathedral (Duomo)

FLORENCE

Leonardo da Vinci Museum

Galileo Museum

"I *wish* we could go faster," says Dovee.

The medallions light up...

...and a gust of wind blows them to a leaning tower.

"Whoa, that was some powerful wind to blow that tower over like that!" says Dovee.

"No, the wind didn't blow it over!" says a dog. "That's the famous leaning tower of Pisa."

"That doesn't look like pizza to me!" says Dovee.

"No, it's not pizza, it's P-I-S-A," the dog replies.

"So why is the tower leaning?" asks Dovee.

"It has been leaning for hundreds of years," says the dog, "because of the unstable ground it was built on."

The dog lifts up his front leg. "Will you take that annoying thing off the bottom of my paw?"

Dan peels a puzzle piece off the dog's paw. The back of this puzzle piece says, "Go to the capital of Italy."

"That's Rome," says the dog.

Dan and Dovee zoom off on their scooter to Rome.

"I *wish* we were in a sports car and I *wish* we could have something cold to eat," moans Dovee.

The medallions light up...

...and they find themselves parked in a red Ferrari by an ice cream stand where they are eating Italian ice cream called gelato.

"This gelato is YUMMY!!" says Dovee. "It's so good!"

Just then a huge seagull swoops down and grabs Dovee's gelato. Something drops from the seagull's foot.

Dan retrieves it and says, "It's another puzzle piece! It says: Go to the island of Capri and you will find the treasure by there."

"Hey Dovee, don't cry."

"..but the seagull stole my gelato!" sobs Dovee.

Dan puts his arm around Dovee and shares his gelato with him.

Dovee and Dan continue on their journey through Rome on their way to Capri.

Colosseum

Gladiator

Pantheon

Spanish Steps

Piazza Navona

Mouth of Truth

Roman Forum

ROME

Trevi Fountain

St. Peter's Basilica The Vatican

"I *wish* I could get my feathers wet!" moans Dovee.

The medallions light up...

...and Dan and Dovee find themselves by the beautiful island of Capri.
"Hey Dovee, get on the yacht. I have something amazing to show you."

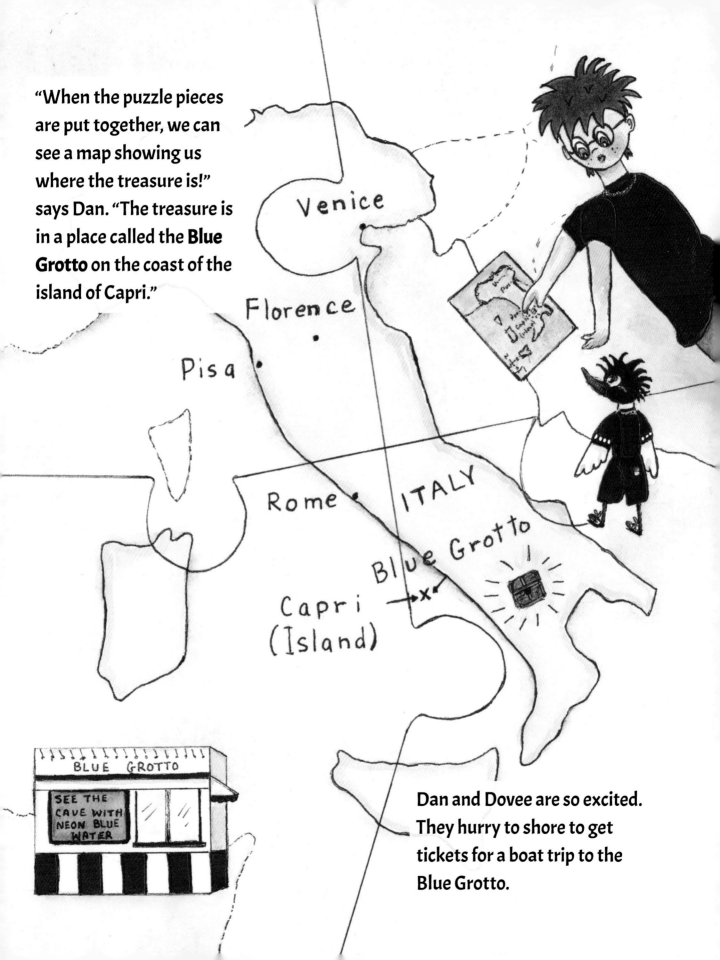

"When the puzzle pieces are put together, we can see a map showing us where the treasure is!" says Dan. "The treasure is in a place called the **Blue Grotto** on the coast of the island of Capri."

Venice

Florence

Pisa

Rome   ITALY

Blue Grotto

Capri
(Island)

BLUE GROTTO

SEE THE
CAVE WITH
NEON BLUE
WATER

Dan and Dovee are so excited. They hurry to shore to get tickets for a boat trip to the Blue Grotto.

When the boat is inside the grotto, Dovee notices bubbles coming from the water and spots a big fish with a key in its mouth. He grabs the key from the fish.

Dovee spots a treasure chest at the bottom of the grotto and dives down to get it.

Dan pulls Dovee and the treasure chest back into the boat.

As soon as they get back on land, Dan impatiently unlocks the treasure chest, curious to see what's inside.

"Wow! Whoopee!" say Dan and Dovee at the same time.

Inside they find gold coins, gondolier outfits, gladiator helmets, new medallions, and a roll of paper.

Dovee unrolls the paper. "Hurray! It's another treasure map!!" he yells excitedly.

"Another adventure! I wonder where this one will take us?" says Dan.

"Why don't we go on our next adventure tomorrow morning?" suggests Dan. "I'm pretty tired and I really miss my family. I *wish* we could go home now."

The medallions light up...